STARLIGHT
SKIN

YOUR COMPLETE GUIDE TO GLOW

KAYE ESCALONA & JESSICA CAMPANA

BALBOA.PRESS
A DIVISION OF HAY HOUSE

Balboa Press books may be ordered through booksellers or by contacting:

Balboa Press
A Division of Hay House
1663 Liberty Drive
Bloomington, IN 47403
www.balboapress.com
1 (877) 407-4847

Because of the dynamic nature of the Internet, any web addresses or links contained in this book may have changed since publication and may no longer be valid. The views expressed in this work are solely those of the author and do not necessarily reflect the views of the publisher, and the publisher hereby disclaims any responsibility for them.

The author of this book does not dispense medical advice or prescribe the use of any technique as a form of treatment for physical, emotional, or medical problems without the advice of a physician, either directly or indirectly. The intent of the author is only to offer information of a general nature to help you in your quest for emotional and spiritual well-being. In the event you use any of the information in this book for yourself, which is your constitutional right, the author and the publisher assume no responsibility for your actions.

Any people depicted in stock imagery provided by Getty Images are models, and such images are being used for illustrative purposes only. Certain stock imagery © Getty Images.

Print information available on the last page.

ISBN: 978-1-9822-5105-5 (sc)
ISBN: 978-1-9822-5151-2 (e)

Balboa Press rev. date: 07/16/2020

CONTENTS

INTRODUCTION

Starlight Skin (adjective): skin that's healthy, smooth, hydrated, and bright. Skin that's so beautiful, its possessor can go makeup-free while still feeling they've got that glow! Starlight skin can be obtained by all, and the knowledge within this book will pave the way.

As co-founders and lead medical estheticians of Starlight Med Spa, we share with you our gathered wisdom from working on thousands of faces with unique characteristics and conditions, spending hours enthralled in dermatological papers and studies, and from transforming our own complexions. Let's begin and get that glow!

CHAPTER 1

STARLIGHT SKIN 101

Let's begin with the "**Starlight Steps**"; a simple template for your daily at-home skincare routine.

Every morning:

1. Cleanse
2. Tone
3. Exfoliate* (where, when, and how often this step falls in your routine depends on multiple factors)
4. Eye Care
5. Serum
6. Moisturize
7. Sun Protection
8. Lip Care
9. Glow Spray

Every night:

1. Remove makeup (if applicable)
2. Cleanse
3. Tone
4. Mask* (Use as needed)
5. Eye Care
6. Serum

7. Moisturize *option to turn this into a richer version of your daytime product
8. Lip care
9. Glow Spray

Cleanse: Removing dirt, excess oil, impurities, and products from your previous application is the foundation of an effective skincare regimen. Cleansing should be thorough and gentle enough to not strip the skin of its natural lipid barrier, which would leave your skin feeling tight. If you avoid a morning facial cleanse because of dehydrated or dry skin you must remember that sweat and grime from hair oils and pillowcases accumulate during the night, and daytime products can't penetrate through last night's old serums and cream. Cleansing twice a day is always a must!

How to: lather your cleanser with warm water and apply with your hands in an upward and outward motion beginning from the chest, going up the neck, and finishing at the forehead. Adding in a gentle mechanical brush made for facial cleansing, gauze, or a microfibre towel can increase the efficiency of the cleansing process. Cleansing techniques vary based on skin types and conditions. If you have oily skin, rosacea, or are acne prone it is important to not overstimulate the skin, which would contribute to increased oil production and aggravation of existing blemishes or sensitive blood vessels. Slow and light pressure should be used in these cases. If you have dry, lackluster, or aging skin firmer pressure and massage movements can be used to invigorate your complexion and stimulate collagen and elastin production while increasing blood flow.

Tone: The role of a toner is to keep the skin's pH level at the balanced state of 5.5 and prepare the skin to absorb products. Maintaining a healthy pH balance in the skin allows it to be calm and ready to execute all reparative functions. Toners can be enhanced to contain exfoliating, hydrating, and nourishing properties to take your regimen to new heights.

How to: apply toner to facial gauze and delicately swipe it across the skin in an upward and outward motion. Start with the face to ensure it gets enough product and finish with the neck and chest as these areas should always be included! Allow the toner to dry before continuing your regimen.

Exfoliate: Exfoliation removes dead skin cells from the surface of the skin allowing active ingredients in products to penetrate to the depths necessary for maximum efficiency. Removing dead skin debris smooths the surface of the skin, allowing light to reflect evenly off the face which creates a radiant look. Exfoliation also allows skin's natural oils to escape the follicle without getting stuck and leading to congestion. Furthermore, the act of exfoliation stimulates fibroblasts in the dermal layer of the skin, which causes these collagen and elastin making machines to increase their productivity, keeping skin firm and youthful. The benefits of exfoliation are endless which is why it's a regular and favorite step in any Glow Getters routine!

How to: choose the right exfoliation medium depending on your skin type, conditions, and desired results.

Mechanical exfoliators include scrubs, brushes, and at-home microdermabrasion systems and must not be overly abrasive or contain particles with sharp edges. Use mechanical exfoliators in upward motions beginning on the chest, moving up the neck, and finishing at the forehead. Apply light pressure on sensitive areas and deeper pressure on areas with rough textures. Avoid the eye area, open lesions, and active acne containing pus. Opening a wound or pimple with this exfoliation method could spread bacteria, delay healing processes, and cause scarring. With scrubs it's optional to cleanse afterwards rather than before to ensure the proper removal of product particles.

Chemical exfoliators often use acidic ingredients to dissolve dead skin cells and unwanted debris on top of or within the skin while speeding up cell turnover rates simultaneously. Common ingredients in these exfoliators include alpha hydroxy acids (AHAs) such as glycolic, lactic, citric, and mandelic acids, and the beta hydroxy acid (BHA) salicylic acid. Chemical exfoliation ingredients can also include enzymes, which are naturally occurring substances that can dissolve dead skin cells. Chemical exfoliators are applied to the skin and are left on or neutralized after a given time based on the strength and potency of the product. These exfoliation ingredients can be used in cleansers, scrubs, gels, serums, and cream products and should be used as the product instructions direct.

Your skin speaks to you and if you learn its language you will always know what it needs. If you're feeling sensitive, reign your exfoliation back until your skin says its okay. If you have a rough texture, enlarged pores, or a dull complexion increase the frequency or strength of your exfoliation regimen.

Take the time to listen to the words of your skin and respond accordingly!

Eye Care: The skin surrounding the eye area is thinner than the skin on the rest of the face. Because of this, the eye area is quick to show signs of aging and needs specialized care. Only products formulated for this area should be used as they contain a gentle and safe concentration of ingredients that should not cause irritation in this delicate place. When the skin near the eye area is hydrated and fed with nutrients it's free to carry out its natural and reparative functions with ease and will remain youthful and plump for a longer period. Eye care must come before serums so that no active ingredients not intended for this thin skin are put here directly.

How to: Apply your eye product underneath the eye with your ring finger, as this finger naturally applies the least amount of pressure. Dab the product from the inner corner of the eye outwards toward the side of the eye. Repeat this step above the lid and move outwards underneath the brow until you reach the side of the eye once more. Always treat your eye area like the most expensive and cherished piece of fine silk!

Serums: Serums contain high concentrations of active ingredients that are intended to correct specific skin issues. They're heavy hitters in any skin expert's regimen and can create visible improvements quickly. Since it's not always clear how different active ingredients may react with others in a separate product, it's generally recommended to use one serum at a time, working on the most important skin issue first, before moving on to the next. Using a serum with a specialized blend to improve multiple conditions at once is also an option. To decrease the risk of a serum's ingredients affecting the efficiency of another using one during the day and the other during the night can also be done. Once you learn your skin's language you can experiment with layering multiple serums at once, being able to adjust and alter your steps if your skin says "no"!

How to: Apply serum to the skin in an upward and outward motion to cover the entire face, neck, and chest. Avoid the eye area unless specified. Specialized serums may be designed for certain areas of the skin only, such as spot treatments designed for acne lesions. Using different serums on different areas of the skin can also be done to customize a routine perfectly. Always follow your serum's specific instructions.

Moisturizer: The role of a moisturizer is to act as a barrier layer on top of the skin, keeping water and the active ingredients of a serum within. Trans-epidermal water loss (TEWL) is the most common reason why skin becomes dehydrated and a great moisturizing seal prevents this. When water levels within the skin are high, all chemical reactions needing H_2O to complete their processes are carried out and the nutritious ingredients in your skincare products are most effective. Skin appears plump, juicy, and full of life!

The barrier a moisturizer creates also protects skin from absorbing potentially pore clogging materials. Such materials may be found in makeup or on the surface of brushes, hands, cell phones, or any other object that may touch the face. A great moisturizer creates a barrier for at least 12 hours. After this timeframe it's important to re-cleanse and reset your regimen.

How to: Apply moisturizer to the skin in an upward and outward motion making sure to include the full face, chest, and neck. During nighttime skincare regimens an additional sealing agent may be applied on top of a regular moisturizer, creating a night cream with a stronger barrier to keep interior hydration levels at their peak. Great sealing agents include pure argan oil and pure shea butter.

Mineral based SPF: Exposure to ultra-violet (UV) rays is the skin's number one extrinsic aging factor. Therefore, all Glow Getters must vow to wear a UV protection product daily and avoid tanning beds like the plague! Limited sun exposure has its benefits and can be enjoyed while wearing protective creams and clothing items to prevent damage to the skin.

Mineral UV protection products typically include titanium dioxide and zinc oxide. These ingredients are accepted as safe and non-toxic to the skin and are recommended by most skincare professionals.

Determining the sun protection factor (SPF) level necessary in a skincare product can be based on the UV index of the climate you're exposed to and the amount of UV exposure expected. Products with a SPF of 30 are generally acceptable for a daily basis.

How to: Apply SPF to the skin in an upward and outward motion being sure to cover the full face, neck, and chest. Include any other areas of the body exposed to UV rays.

During periods of prolonged UV exposure reapply SPF every two hours.

Lip Care: As a Glow Getter your lips must always be as hydrated as your radiant face. Lips must be exfoliated and moisturized with products meant for this area on a regular basis!

How to: With gentle, circular motions massage lip exfoliator into the lips until all unwanted debris is removed and lips are ready to receive their hydration product. Follow with your favorite nutritious lip balm.

Glow Spray: Skincare finishing sprays are meant to add a final burst of hydration, and make you feel amazing about the great work you've just done! Sprays can leave you with a mattified or luminous finishing depending on the formula's intention.

How to: Spray the mist finely over areas to be hydrated. Respray throughout the day as needed.

Removing Makeup: Removing makeup properly decreases the risk of eye irritations, keeps lashes in supreme condition, and prepares the surface of the skin for the deep cleanse that follows. It also ensures your pillowcase stays the colour it was meant to be!

How to: Carefully remove makeup with a gentle product designed for this purpose. The product may be applied with dampened gauze, cotton, or a microfibre material. Continue patiently and with light pressure until no more makeup residue is detected.

Masks: Masks have specialized functions and come in a variety of forms such as creams, gels, powders, pre-soaked sheets, and clays. They can be incorporated into the Starlight Steps as needed, when extra time is available, or to bring the in-spa facial experience home!

How to: Apply mask to face, neck, and chest if it's meant for general health and hydration. To enhance the experience a fine bristled brush may be used to spread the product. With masks intended to absorb excess oil or to calm acne lesions apply to areas where oil or congestion is present only. Powdered masks can be enhanced by mixing them with antioxidant rich, caffeine free teas or water with antibacterial agents like apple cider vinegar or tea tree oil lightly added. Follow the specific directions of your mask and feel free to re-tone the skin before proceeding to the next Starlight Steps if needed.

So, there you have it, a Glow Getter template for your at home regimen! Now all you must do is identify your skin's type and conditions to select the right products to reach your goals. As you gain confidence in your skincare knowledge and learn to listen to what your skin tells you, you'll be able to further customize your routine. Skincare is an art and knowing when and why to use which products comes with practice and observation!

CHAPTER 2

STARLIGHT'S PRODUCT PHILOSOPHY

The Starlight Steps lay the foundation for your skincare practice, but there are a few crucial things about products you must know.

1. Products in your regimen must contain ingredients that are scientifically proven to make a difference in the skin. We want visible results not just empty promises written on a bottle! Look for studies done by the skincare company you are purchasing from and independently research the ingredients.

2. Products in your regimen must be formulated without the use of unnatural perfumes, coloring agents, or unnecessary additives. By using products free of these, the risks of irritation and affecting the efficiency of active ingredients is reduced! The sacrifice of pretty fragrances and coloured creams will be well worth it when you're glowing brighter than ever!

3. Products in your regimen must be non-comedogenic, meaning they will not sit within the pore or hair follicle and clog it, backtracking all skin transformation progress! Using pore clogging ingredients unknowingly is the number one reason many suffer with congestion

despite committing to a full skincare routine. It's rare to find any product on the market whose ingredient list scores zeros across the board, on the comedogenic scale. Many professional products tailored towards acne-prone skin are actually loaded with ingredients that have the potential to cause breakouts.

The comedogenic scale is a rating system 0-5 of an ingredient's ability to clog a pore. This scale was developed in the eighties by dermatologists but was never uniformly accepted because their studies were conducted on the ears of rabbits, instead of human skin. Critics claimed that human facial skin responds differently and that some of the ingredients rating on the scale have anti-congestion properties. Because of this the comedogenic rating system was disregarded by most and never added to dermatology or esthetic educational curriculums.

Starlight discovered the comedogenic scale to be true after years in the esthetics industry, from constant research to determine why many skins weren't clearing despite following strict product and treatment regimens. After carefully monitoring the ingredients in all products recommended and in treatment formulas, Starlight noticed a definite reduction in client breakouts and in "product induced milia" when ingredients rating high on the comedogenic scale were removed. Product induced milia is different than a whitehead. The substance inside this lesion is thick and oozes out like toothpaste in a squeeze-tube when extracted. Smaller versions of product induced milia can easily be seen in the thin-skinned undereye area and are often unextractable. Soon after the revelation of the comedogenic scale it became easy to tell which clients used pore-clogging products just by taking a quick glance at the skin underneath the eye and areas of acne for the presence of these tiny, hard, and white congestions that form from pore clogging product substances.

To check the comedogenic ratings in a product enter each ingredient in an internet search engine alongside "comedogenic scale". For most ingredients you will find a score between 0-5. 0 means the ingredient will not clog a pore and 5 means it most certainly will. All ratings in between cause a small to high risk as the number increases. Pore clogging ingredients lead to acne in those prone, enlarged pores in those who naturally secrete oils, and product induced milia in almost everyone. By abiding to the comedogenic scale you increase your chances of getting the skin of your dreams. Even though many skincare professionals and product manufacturers are not aware of the comedogenic scale, by following this system you lower the risk of reversing the progress of your efforts and wasting your money.

CHAPTER 3

SKIN TYPES AND CONDITIONS

Knowing your skin's type and conditions allows you to carefully select the products you'll need to fulfill your daily Starlight Steps!

Skin Types

Your skin type is determined by the amount and location of your skin's sebaceous (sebum; oil) secretions. Skin types may change throughout a lifetime due to changes in the body's hormone levels.

Dry Skin: Dry skin does not produce oils naturally. Skin remains matte and shine free throughout the day unless a sheen is created by a product. Dry skin is prone to premature creping and wrinkling, as it lacks lipids found in sebum that enhance elasticity and moisture. If you have dry skin, products containing oils or rich lubricants that do not register on the comedogenic scale are recommended.

Oily Skin: Oily skin produces sebum regularly and begins to display an all over sheen as the day progresses. If you have oily skin, products free of oils and rich lubricants should be used to prevent the skin from appearing overly glossy. It is especially important that no ingredients registering on the comedogenic scale are used if you have this skin type, as your risk of congestion is great.

Combination Skin: Combination skin has areas of the face that produce oils and areas that do not. The sebum rich areas are typically found in the t-zone and include the forehead, nose, and chin. If you have this skin type, products containing a light, balanced amount of oils or lubricants not registering on the comedogenic scale or products containing ingredients with high hydration properties if oil-free are recommended. Using different products in the areas with different skin types is an alternative way to make sure your skin looks its best.

Normal Skin: This type of skin has a balanced and efficient amount of sebum and the skin's acid mantle has a perfectly leveled pH of 5.5. Lucky you, your skin seems to always look great with minimal effort! If you have this skin type use products with high amounts of healthy, youth promoting ingredients, and experiment with non-comedogenic oils to make your complexion even more lustrous.

The Fitzpatrick Scale

The Fitzpatrick scale is a casting system determined by an individual's response to ultra-violet (UV) rays, which allows professionals to determine appropriate machine settings when working with photo technologies and allows you to further classify your skin type. Awareness of your skin's characteristics helps you understand skin conditions and risks you may face in your skincare lifetime.

Type 1: Type 1s have the fairest complexion pigment-wise. If you're a type 1 you burn quickly when exposed to UV rays and struggle to achieve a tan. You're prone to sun damage, rosacea, and may show premature signs of aging skin. Type 1s are typically of northern European decent and may freckle easily.

Type 2: Type 2s have a fair complexion and burn in the sun. They can achieve a tan after the burn fades. Skin type 2s are of northern to mid European decent and could have lightly pigmented eyes. If you're a skin type 2 you may experience premature signs of aging and are more prone to rosacea than the following skin types.

Type 3: Type 3s have a fair to beige skin tone and are most commonly of European decent. When exposed to UV light type 3s may freckle and occasionally burn but can achieve an overall attractive tan. If you're a type 3 you respond well to phototherapy skincare procedures and have no extra risks associated with treatments.

Type 4: Skin type 4s have an olive or light brown skin tone, usually with golden undertones. This skin type almost never burns and always tans. Type 4s may be of southern Mediterranean, middle eastern, or Asian decent. If you're a type 4 you face an increased risk of hyperpigmentation from skincare treatments done with incorrect settings, acne lesions, and general traumas to the skin.

Type 5: Skin type 5s have a caramel coloured complexion, sun insensitive skin, and rarely burn from UV exposure. Skin type 5s may be of Indian, middle eastern, or African decent. If you're a skin type 5 you face higher risks of hyperpigmentation, hypopigmentation, and burns from photo and skincare treatments done incorrectly. You may also be prone to keloid scarring if your skin is injured. Because of this, do your due diligence research on machinery used and the experience of the skincare technician when considering professional skin procedures.

Type6: Skin type 6s have a deeply pigmented complexion and never burn when exposed to UV rays. Type 6s are typically of Indian or African decent and must use caution when undergoing photo and skincare treatments due to the high levels of melanin in the skin. If you're a skin type 6 you face the highest chance of injury from skincare treatments gone wrong. You must therefore align yourself with a skincare professional you trust and always take the time to understand associated treatment risks.

Skin Conditions

Skin conditions are changeable factors your skin may experience and include acne and imperfect texture, rosacea, hyperpigmentation, dehydration, and premature aging. If you have several skin conditions at once it may be best to clear them individually beginning with the one that affects you most or you may strategize your routine to clear several simultaneously!

ACNE: LET'S GET CLEAR

Acne is the inflammation and infection that occurs when excess, or thicker sebum (oil) builds up in a closed off hair follicle (blocked by dead skin cells or unnatural debris), and p. acne bacteria begins to grow and multiply within the follicle. Acne can consist of a variety of lesions such as a papule (red bump), a pustule (red bump with white, pus-filled head), a cyst (an enlarged and painful papule, that is the result of walls collapsing between the separate hair follicles), blackheads (excess sebum and debris built up within the follicle, and oxidized by the air), and whiteheads (excess sebum and debris built up within the follicle).

Causes of Acne:

Although the main cause of acne stems from your genetic make up, there are three factors responsible for the formation of this stubborn condition that we're able to address:

1. **Increased or excess sebum**: This can be caused by your body's androgens (male hormones) triggering sebum production in reaction to stress, monthly body cycles, certain foods, or medications. Excess oil can also be caused by applying them topically onto the skin during your daily skincare regimen, and by overstimulating the skin.

Starlight Tips:

Keeping daily stress as low as possible is important in regulating sebum production. Some helpful tools in this area include meditation and quieting the mind, affirmations, exercise, planning and executing tasks in a timely manner as opposed to procrastination, and living in the moment instead of worrying about past or future scenarios that are out of your control. These actions and mind states require practice and persistence, but your efforts will be rewarded with a clearer complexion amongst countless other benefits.

Having your hormone levels checked by a respected naturopath, endocrinologist, or doctor is another avenue worth exploring to regulate sebum production. Your healthcare professional may make reasonable recommendations to harmonize your hormones and control your acne lesions. Always do your own research and follow through with actions that feel comfortable to you.

Ensuring that all ingredients in your skincare products do not register on the comedogenic scale is necessary in keeping skin oils in check. When fighting acne, the general rule of thumb is to go oil-free with products since your body is producing more than enough oil on its own. If your acneic skin feels tight or is flaking it is due to dehydration of the epidermis, which is a separate condition where the skin lacks water. Alternatively, if you're a dry skin type who is experiencing acne or congestion of the skin in the form of tiny white bumps beneath the skin's surface (product-induced milia), it's certain that the condition is caused by oils or ingredients foreign to your body, as oil is not produced naturally within your hair follicles. This type of milia is easiest to see in the thin skin surrounding the undereye area, and when you gently stretch the skin apart with your fingers. To remove any type of unwanted oil, masks with a clay base work wonders to sop up any excess residues and can be used daily if necessary.

Be sure to not overstimulate acneic skin with microcurrent devices, energizing ingredients such as caffeine, vitamin C, and peppermint, and invigorating facial massage, as all of these can lead to an increased surge of sebum. Inflamed lesions require calming actions only, and if obtaining a more youthful complexion is a parallel goal, some anti-aging methods may have to wait until this condition is controlled.

The final way to prevent sebum production from going overboard is by decreasing dairy, soy, and meats from animals treated with steroids or hormones in your diet, as foods containing these substances have been shown to alter the body's androgen levels in several conclusive studies.

2. **Blocked hair follicles**: This may be caused by dead skin cell build-up due to lack of exfoliation, retention hyperkeratosis (a hereditary factor where dead skin cells stick together and do not slough off naturally), or by excess debris from dirt, makeup, or objects making contact with the face.

Starlight Tips:

Frequent exfoliation is critical in keeping follicles unobstructed. By constantly removing dead skin cells as they come to the surface of the skin, sebum will always be free to exit the skin without issue. Salicylic acid is the primary chemical used to keep pores clean as it is oil soluble and can do its work effectively within the oily pore. Other acids and methods of exfoliation should be used to remove the more superficial blockages. Be careful of physical exfoliation if you have pustules, as they can be ripped open in the process causing deep scarring and spreading bacteria. Exfoliate often and listen to what your skin is telling you. If you are over-exfoliating you will begin to feel skin sensitivity and it will be time to adjust your regimen and reduce this skincare step.

Using a retinol serum in your nightly Starlight Steps is another great way to keep your pores clear. Retinol is an ingredient derived from vitamin A and is a magical skincare ingredient that is recommended throughout a Glow Getter's lifetime. Retinol speeds up cell turnover and improves the rate at which dead skin cells slough of the skin's surface. This means it can produce several amazing results which include an even, acne-free complexion. Adding retinol to your regimen requires an adjustment period where you may face "the retinol uglies"! This "ugly phase" where your skin gets used to this impactful ingredient may include flaking skin, a rough texture, and even new cycles of vicious acne. Rest assured and stay strong, your persistent devotion to getting on retinol will be well worth it in the long run.

In addition to always using non-comedogenic products, keeping all things that may contact the face daily free of greasy residue and bacteria is essential in complexion perfection. These items may include hands, telephones, pillowcases, makeup brushes, and glasses. Stick to a regular cleansing schedule of these potential acne inducers and consider sleeping with your hair wrapped unless you can go non-comedogenic with your styling products as well.

Permanently reducing facial hair with laser hair removal can also be an effective way to keep the follicles open and free, as this will remove one potential clogger from the situation while preventing the existence of ingrown hair congestion.

3. **The presence of P. acne bacteria at the base of the hair follicle:** Propionibacterium acne is the bacteria inside the pore that multiplies and causes the infection and inflammation associated with acne. This bacterium is anaerobic, meaning it cannot survive if oxygen is present. Therefore, if the opening to the hair follicle is kept unblocked through exfoliation air can flow through and your acne lesion will not inflate. On top of this further actions can be done to execute this pesky multiplier.

<u>Starlight Tips:</u>

LED therapy is a staple in the good-skin game and when it comes to acne, blue light is a pimple's worst nightmare. Blue light emits a wavelength of 400-495nm and penetrates to the level beneath the skin where p. acne bacteria resides. When blue light and this bacterium meet, phosphates react, and the bacteria is killed. At-home blue light devices are recommended daily if acne is persistent and come in a variety of hand-held and hands-free options. 10-minute sessions are recommended. Always follow the specific directions of your blue light device.

High frequency current is also able to eradicate pesky p. acne bacteria and is no longer left to the professional skin specialist only. Your high frequency wand should be used in a "sparking" motion on top of the acne lesion, by lifting the tip of the wand on and off the skin in a repetitive motion. The frequency of the wand works wonders, as it can change surrounding oxygen molecules into "ozone", which is what produces that refreshing "after rain" aroma in the air when you use it. Ozone is an anti-bacterial agent able to assist in clearing the breakout fast. Use your high frequency wand two times daily for your best result.

Specific ingredients in the skincare industry are known to reduce and kill acne causing bacteria and include benzoyl peroxide, witch hazel, sulphur, and tea-tree oil. Try one of these ingredients in your serum or spot treatment. High concentrations of these ingredients can contribute to dehydration, so make sure to take steps to maintain a high-water content in the epidermis to maintain your glow.

The Links Between Your Diet and Acne:

Foods which cause an inflammatory response to the body can make the skin swell, resulting in easily clogged pores. Foods which alter hormone levels can cause an increase in the skin's oil production and make the chance of an acne lesion more likely. On the contrary the right foods can skyrocket you to gaining your ultimate glow. Your body is unique, so the relationship between it and food may differ from the experience of others.

<u>Starlight Tips</u>:

Begin an elimination diet and record your findings to see if certain food groups (the main ones are wheat/gluten, sugars, dairy, processed foods, and caffeine) contribute to the state of your skin. Stick to your diet, as changes can take time. It will get easier and it will be worth it!

1. **Gluten**: experiment with removing this protein from your diet.

   Many people have a sensitivity to gluten and are unaware. Gluten sensitivity can lead to digestion problems, which can lead to unstable hormones, and increased oil (more acne!).

   Brown rice, natural and unsweetened oatmeal, brown rice pasta, quinoa, lentils, and beans are all examples of gluten-free carbohydrates.

2. **Sugar**: reduce sugars in your diet. Sugars are inflammatory to your body's systems and can swell the skin, reducing the pore size of the follicle and making blockages more likely. This inflammation can also make existing acne redder and angrier than it already is. When regulating your sugar consumption, it's essential to understand food labels, as added sugar is a common thing. Preparing your own food at home ensures you know exactly what it contains and will help you to keep the sugars low. Avoid processed and simple carbohydrates as they are quickly converted into sugar through your body's natural digestive process. Alcoholic beverages are another thing to be weary of

in the pursuit of clear skin, as they are typically full of sugar. Limit your drinks, and if necessary, go with a clear liquor mixed with sparkling water and a spritz of citrus fruit. Drink in moderation, as you would never want to pass out without doing your nightly skincare regimen (or many other horrible situations). Although fruits are natural and full of health properties, they are still comprised of sugar. Limit your fruit intake until you figure out your path to clear skin. Berries in moderation are usually your best choice if fruit is a must for you.

3. **Dairy**: A lactating animal is full of hormones, and some studies show consuming dairy can affect our own hormones, causing increased or thicker oil production. Reduce dairy as much as possible and find dairy substitutes that work for you. Unsweetened almond milk or other sugar-free, nut-based milk are wonderful dairy substitutes. Coconut milk is another delicious dairy substitute, but its higher sugar content can make it a less effective clear skin choice. Be wary of soy products, as soy has been linked to having hormone altering effects when consumed regularly. Experiment with vegan cheeses and yogurts, and if you aren't a fan of substitutes limit dairy as much as possible.

4. **Processed food**: A diet full of processed, refined, and chemically altered food deprives you of the proper nutrients your skin needs to look its best, and can contribute to your body's state of inflammation, swelling the skin and increasing the risk of acne. Eating a variety

of nutrient dense, fresh, and natural vegetables, whole grains, and proteins is recommended for Starlight Skin.

5. **Caffeine:** If you have naturally oily and acneic skin caffeine can contribute to an increase in congestion by stimulating your sebaceous glands to produce more oil. Reducing or eliminating caffeine by consuming plentiful amounts of purified water and antioxidant rich, caffeine-free teas is the Glow Getter way!

With knowing all the links between what you eat and the clearness of your complexion it's essential to remember that being happy and fulfilled in life always comes first. Food is a joyous and spiritual experience and if limiting and changing your diet makes you less happy, then work at perfecting the other suggested ways of obtaining flawless skin to compensate. This diet strategy should always be done in a balanced way that leaves you free of guilt and unnecessary stress.

Pimple Popping 101:

Popping any lesion that is not "ready to pop" will automatically result in a long-lasting, dark-pigmented scar. Learn to have restraint and only pop if a large, white head is present within the pimple. Blackheads and whiteheads may be carefully extracted after exfoliation and skin steaming, from your shower or steaming device. Self-extraction isn't for everyone, and if your face ends up with more damage and scarring than before you began, leave this step to the professional.

1. Begin with a sterilized or 1 use lancet. You can purchase these from a drug-store's diabetic product section. Make sure your hands are clean.
2. Poke a tiny hole in the white head, using only the tip of the lancet and feather-light pressure.
3. Use a professional, sanitized extractor tool to apply gradual pressure to the sides of the pimple surrounding the tiny hole you created. Sanitize with alcohol wipes or an at-home autoclave.
4. Drain the pimple until no more white pus is present.
5. Kill any p.acne bacteria that may have been spread by this extraction by cleansing your face and applying a anti-bacterial spot treatment to the area, doing a blue-light LED therapy session, or zapping the skin with a high frequency device.

Sebum Filaments

If you have oily or acne prone skin you've likely noticed tiny whitehead-like clogs always present in the sides of the nose and in the chin, just underneath the bottom lip, no matter how well and how often you extract. These stubborn congestions are sebum filaments and are a sign that your skin is producing sebum. Filaments will exist in oily or combination skins until hormonal changes alter the skin's type over time and the skin changes to dry.

Enlarged Pores

Visibly enlarged pores are the result of overly abundant sebum production or comedogenic ingredients sitting within the skin for a sustained period. The first step towards shrinking a pore is removing the excess residue that's inside so the pore is free to close. This can be done with salicylic acid and products with a clay base. Next the skin must be resurfaced from above through exfoliation and cell turnover must be sped up from below. Starlight's favorite way to speed up cell turnover is with retinol. Medical spa treatments have many advanced techniques and treatments to diminish pore size and should be utilized for quicker results.

Professional Skin Clearing Treatments:

Many professional treatments can help clear active acne and the scarring left behind much faster than if left untouched. Common, effective acne treatments include deep exfoliation and resurfacing done with chemical peeling and microdermabrasion, fractional-ablation and microneedling where controlled injury triggers the production of collagen, elastin, and new skin cells to improve scarred textures, and blue-light lasers and intense pulsed light that stop p.acne bacteria growth in its tracks. It's important to understand the science, risks, protocols, and aftercare associated with any treatment you plan to undergo, as well as to diligently research the brands of technology the skin clinic uses to get your best and safest result. Pairing your medical spa plan with dietary and supplementation guidance from a natural medical practitioner can skyrocket your skincare success even further.

Prescription Medications to Treat the Skin

In rare cases after a perfect and consistent effort has been applied towards a flawless, clear canvas medications prescribed by a dermatologist may be considered to make you acne-free. Doctors have access to strong ingredients that can exfoliate, speed up cell turnover, kill p.acne bacteria, and subdue an overactive sebaceous gland, however, these products and pills almost always go hand in hand with skin dehydration and even serious risks to your overall health. Following the Starlight Steps, lowering stress, thinking positive clear skin thoughts, and following a Glow Getter diet can get you a radiant complexion risk-free and is therefore recommended first.

ROSACEA: LET'S CALM DOWN

Rosacea is a skin condition in which several blood vessels become dilated, enlarged, and in some cases, break causing visible flushing of the skin. This condition is commonly associated with skin sensitivity and small, red bumps or skin irritation.

What causes rosacea?

In most cases Mom and Dad can be thanked for passing on the trait of weaker and superficial blood vessels, but there are also many extrinsic factors that can cause these vessels to enlarge and become damaged.

1. **Ultra-violet rays**: especially UVA rays, which penetrate deeply to reach the dermal layer of the skin, are a primary factor in causing rosacea and making the existing condition worse.

Starlight tips:

Wearing a mineral-based SPF of 30 or higher every day is a must. Even in cold and stormy conditions UVA rays penetrate through clouds and windows. Never commit the skincare sin of frying your blood vessels in a tanning bed, as these beds are 95% or more UVA based. They're guaranteed to back-track your quest towards an even complexion, and with so many safe self-tanning options are becoming a thing of the past. In climates with a high UV index up your sun protection factor and be sure to reapply your SPF on a bi-hourly basis. Remember to invest in some stylish hats and other protective accessories to ensure Starlight Skin status for a lifetime.

2. **Dermal trauma**: Trauma to the upper layer of the dermis can cause blood vessels to become damaged.

Starlight tips:

Avoid aggressive forms of exfoliation such as mechanical exfoliation with non-spherical beads like gritty nut scrubs, which can cause microtears with their jagged edges. Lactic acid is a wise exfoliation choice for those with rosy complexions, as it's the most gentle AHA. Treat your skin gently whenever possible, and care for it as you would the most expensive and luxurious piece of silk.

When it comes to the extraction of blemishes go in with an easy hand to avoid lasting capillary damage which may be worse than the pimple itself.

3. **Other factors** which can lead to rosacea and flare current symptoms include excessive alcohol consumption, spicy food, stimulants such as caffeine, inflammatory agents such as sugar, vigorous exercise, mental stress, exposure to high heat, skincare products containing fragrance or colouring and medications which increase blood pressure or dilate vessels.

Starlight tips:

Be observant of the state of your rosacea after consuming specific foods and beverages. Eliminate or reduce any of these triggers to avoid excess pressure on your fragile capillaries. Since exercise is essential to a Glow Getter's lifestyle, consider forms that elevate your blood flow in interval rates and get your workout done in a cooler climate setting. Stress negatively impacts your skin in various ways and can cause increased blood pressure, which is an enemy of a calm complexion. To stay calm when stress creeps in focus on present moment solutions instead of past emotions and fear of future scenarios and remember to breathe deeply. When it comes to your shower routine opt out of those steaming hot sessions and reduce the heat to a temperature that's still enjoyable. Saunas and steam rooms should be limited or crossed off your list of leisurely activities completely. Use skincare products free of unnecessary scents and dyes, and take care of your mind, body, and soul to the best of your ability to reduce the risk of needing medications that may aggravate your skin.

Managing and Treating Rosacea:

1. **Restore the skin's lipid barrier:** Strengthening and repairing the skin's lipid barrier, a protective film that builds on top of the epidermis to keep external irritants from penetrating, is vital in obtaining calm skin. You can build up your skin's natural shield by avoiding harsh astringents with high concentrations of alcohol, supplementing daily with essential fatty acids, keeping skin's hydration and nutrient levels elevated with serums, and enclosing the epidermis with a rich, emollient based moisturizer. Common skin calming ingredients that are great in anti-redness products include aloe, vitamin E, niacinamide, squalene, hyaluronic acid, and arnica. Adding an additional seal to your moisturizer at night, such as argan oil or pure shea butter will assist in creating a strong, ceramide effect to lessen sensitivities.

2. **Red-light therapy**: Regular use of red-light therapy is proven to have an anti-inflammatory and regenerative effect on the skin's dermal layer, where blood vessels reside. It can strengthen and repair capillary walls, as well as the

additional benefit of increasing collagen and elastin proteins through fibroblast stimulation. 20 minutes a day, 5 times per week is suggested, but there is no such thing as too much red light. The extensive benefits are well worth this extra effort, and you can listen to your favorite meditation to reduce stress simultaneously. Since LED therapy is a common occurrence in a Glow Getter's skincare routine, it's best to use a dome-like device to ensure comfort during use, instead of LED masks, which can feel heavy on the face. Always remember your protective eyewear during any light therapy.

3. **Laser and Intense Pulsed Light (IPL):** Laser and IPL treatments use a targeted and controlled pulse of energy to destroy superficial, broken blood vessels. They are the go-to treatment in the esthetics industry to dramatically improve the appearance of rosacea and yield impressive results when performed with quality machinery. It's essential that you follow the prerequisite and after care advice of your trusted medical spa technician and clinic when undergoing any form of phototherapy.

HYPERPIGMENTATION: LET'S GET EVEN

Hyperpigmentation is the darkening of skin colour because of excess melanin production. The only case where hyperpigmentation does not equate to UV damage or overworked melanocytes is natural freckling that's present from a young age. Freckling that appears in the late teenage years and beyond is a result of continuous exposure to UV light and is called "solar lentigo". When skin darkens or scars because of trauma to the skin, from a wound or acne lesion, it's known as "post inflammatory hyperpigmentation" (PIH). When hyperpigmentation occurs in patterned marks because of hormonal changes it's known as "melasma". Regardless of the origin, the treatment methods to fade these unwanted marks are the same.

What Causes Hyperpigmentation to Form?

Hyperpigmentation forms when the body's natural enzyme, tyrosinase, triggers the melanocytes to formulate excess melanin when stimulated by UV radiation, damage to the epidermis, or hormones.

How to Prevent & Treat Hyperpigmentation

Starlight tips:

Avoid all forms of excess UV exposure, including artificial lamps. When exposed to natural sunlight, cover up with clothing and a hat. Mineral-based sunscreen with a UV protection rating of at least 30 should be worn daily and reapplied every two hours when in direct sunlight with a high UV index. The days of frying your skin to achieve your maximum level of golden brown are over! It's time to invest in a great self-tanner.

Controlling active acne is crucial to prevent a continuous cycle of hyperpigmentation. Apply your newfound Starlight Skin knowledge of how to clear your complexion and abstain from picking lesions unless the pus-filled white head is begging you to properly pop it according to Starlight's rules of extraction.

Persistent exfoliation to slough off the top layer of pigmented skin reveals a fresher and more uniform complexion. Exfoliation also speeds up the cell-turnover process, which slows as we age. This means the pigmented skin will move towards the surface where it eventually can be exfoliated off much faster. An effective retinol night serum can be used as a separate addition to your mechanical or chemical exfoliant to speed up this process.

Regular use of green light LED therapy has been shown to decrease dark spots with time, although the science behind its efficacy is not as conclusive as red and blue light. Regardless, using this tool can only help you reach your skin goals as quickly as possible! Give it a go and commit to a ten-minute LED therapy session each day.

Using skincare products with ingredients that can block the tyrosinase enzyme from functioning stops its signal from reaching the melanocytes, and much less excess melanin is created due to UV exposure, PIH, or hormonal triggers. These ingredients are most often found in serums and include:

1. Hydroquinone: the gold-standard, medical-grade ingredient which effectively decreases hyperpigmentation. Hydroquinone is a controversial ingredient in the beauty industry, as some studies have shown it to register on toxicity scales. Hydroquinone is FDA approved in 2% or lower quantity and should only be used if all applicable risks are accepted.

2. Vitamin C: a natural antioxidant that has proven brightening abilities and can decrease excess melanin production with consistent use.

3. Kojic acid: derived from fungi, kojic acid has been proven to decrease hyperpigmentation with time.

4. Azelaic acid: this acid can decrease melanocyte activity, decreasing pigmentation surpluses especially when used in 20% strength or greater.

Professional Medical Spa Treatments for an Even Complexion

1. **Laser & Intense pulsed light (IPL):** Laser and IPL are one of the most effective ways to quickly diminish excess pigment when performed correctly. These treatments penetrate a controlled beam of light into the epidermal layers of the skin and cause excess melanin to break down and be absorbed by the body.

2. **Skin resurfacing by chemical peeling**: Chemical peeling can be customized in strength and by acid type depending on the skin's tone, texture, and special needs. Chemical peeling works by exfoliating the superficial layers of the epidermis while simultaneously speeding up cell turnover. Strong, chemical peeling can result in the physical shedding of the skin's outermost layers in the days following the procedure.

3. **Skin resurfacing through professional mechanical exfoliation**: Mechanical exfoliation is a conservative approach to pigment lightening as it lowers the associated treatment risks for those with naturally darker complexions. Herbal peeling is an example of this and can create similar results to chemical peels. Microdermabrasion is the most popular form of mechanical exfoliation as it involves no client down-time in most cases.

4. **Fractional or full ablation treatments**: Treatments involving fractional or full ablation decrease hyperpigmentation along with several other skin conditions, making them extremely effective professional treatments. Ablation is defined as the removal of skin tissue. Ablation triggers the body's natural response to repair controlled damage by producing mass amounts of collagen and elastin fibres creating new and fresh skin. Ablation is typically done with laser, radio frequency waves, or microneedles.

   It's important to note that light, resurfacing, and ablation treatments make the skin photo-sensitive meaning it becomes even more sensitive to ultra-violet radiation. The use of great sun-protection products is always essential alongside treating existing hyperpigmentation. Be aware of treatment risks, prerequisites, and down time instructions before undergoing treatment with the skin professional you trust.

What is Hypopigmentation?

Hypopigmentation is the loss of melanin in the skin due to epidermal trauma, UV damage, or autoimmune disorders such as vitiligo. Hypopigmentation appears as patches of blanched skin and is not easily corrected. If hypopigmentation is the result of dermal trauma it may be temporary and you can aid in its recovery by speeding up cell turnover with retinols, microcurrents, and medical spa treatments, while simultaneously sloughing off the superficial dead skin cell layer with frequent exfoliation. Semi-permanent or permanent dermal tattooing is also an option that could be considered in treating hypopigmentation.

DEHYDRATION: LET'S GET DEWY

Dehydrated skin lacks water in the epidermal tissue and is independent from dry skin, the skin type lacking natural oils, that it's often confused with. Dehydrated skin manifests as a dull, crepe-like, flaky texture and can be experienced by anyone, regardless of skin type or other present skin conditions.

How Does Skin Lose its Water Content?

Water within the skin is continuously lost through trans-epidermal water loss (TEWL). This means water is pulled out of the skin into the external environment, especially during colder seasons when humidity levels are low. Natural perspiration throughout the day or during physical activity is also a predominant factor in TEWL.

Why is it important to have a high moisture content in the epidermal layers?

Aside from the "dewy" and youthful appearance that's associated with hydrated skin, chemical reactions occurring within the epidermis (and the body) need H_2O to complete their functions. This means for your skin to work at optimal levels it must be full of moisture!

Can you imagine the visual difference of dehydrated grass and grass that's been regularly watered? The later radiates a vibrant colour, a healthy texture, and is a thriving expression of life. Your skin will acquire these same traits once you take the correct measures to maintain its hydration levels.

How to Keep Your Skin Hydrated:

Starlight tips:

Aim to drink 2-3L of purified water each day to help your skin and body thrive! Think of water as your "glow elixir" and flavor it with citrus, cucumber, or mint to make it even more delicious. Adding a collagen powder to your beauty drink can also be a smart addition. Remember to up your water quantities when consuming dehydrating beverages like coffee or alcohol!

Exfoliating on a regular basis so your skin can accept the hydrating ingredients in your products is paramount in creating a dewy glow! Ingredients are unable to penetrate through a wall of chunky, dead skin cells, so without removing this layer any serums and moisturizers will remain superficial and be ineffective. The penetration of ingredients with water-binding properties into the lower depths of the skin is a Glow Getter's best hydration trick! Common high-humectant and non-comedogenic ingredients include hyaluronic acid and squalane. When your serums are still moist on the skin is a great time to use a microcurrent, ultrasonic, or high-frequency device as these energies can assist in product penetration through their vibrational movements. Be sure that the serums used alongside these devices do not have highly stimulating ingredients such as AHAs or retinols, as combining the two can cause skin irritation.

Once your skin has been flooded with nutrition from your water-binding serums it's time to create a seal with a great moisturizer! The role of a moisturizer is to serve as an occlusive barrier, keeping important ingredients within the skin and preventing internal water from being lost through TEWL. A moisturizer's secondary function is to protect the skin from external factors and irritants, which improves skin sensitivities and strengthens the epidermal lipid barrier. During lower-humidity seasons or for extremely dehydrated skin, an additional barrier can be added on top of a moisturizer to create a thicker, and more effective hydration seal. A great idea for this second barrier is argan oil, a natural oil that does not register on the comedogenic scale. This can be done during nighttime regimens only if the additional barrier is too thick, or shiny for some skin types during the day.

Adding humidifiers to your house or bedroom, especially during lower-humidity seasons is an additional Starlight tip to keep you glowing! If there are high levels of water molecules present in the air, the chance of water being pulled from the skin is much less. Those long, hot showers and baths you love may also need to be reduced, as steaming water breaks down the skin's lipid barrier and adds to the dehydration of your face and body. Follow the same Starlight advice to keep a hydrated face when it comes to the skin on your body. Start with a great body moisturizer to seal in the water from your shower and then apply a sealing oil on top! Both face and body hydration products are designed to last for an average period of 12 hours, so reapplication after this time is necessary on all body parts to keep your radiance at 100%. If areas such as the elbows, knees, and feet still aren't as radiant as you would like, add on our favorite rich seal, natural shea-butter for a quick improvement! Shea butter is also a great ingredient to keep atopic dermatitis that coincides with dehydrated skin, such as eczema, under control instead of resorting to medical steroid products.

Are Night-Creams Necessary?

Night creams contain richer occlusive barriers than your daytime moisturizer to keep water within the skin. This can make them appear too "greasy" or shiny to be worn in the daytime. Since most night creams register on the comedogenic scale because of these rich ingredients, they could also result in clogged pores, blemishes, enlarged pore size, and little white bumps underneath the skin's surface called "product induced milia". Because of this Starlight recommends using argan oil to create the additional seal instead of investing in a separate cream for night if your goal is hydration. Night creams with specialized ingredients that cause photosensitivity, such as retinol are recommended for use during the dark hours only. During the night skin repairs itself, so some night creams may contain select ingredients that are intended to aid your skin in this natural function and can be a complimentary addition to your Starlight Steps. As always be sure that your products fit in with Starlight's product philosophy: proven to work, no unnecessary fragrance or dyes, and non-comedogenic.

In-Spa Treatments for Hydrated Skin

The best professional treatments for dehydrated skin often involve a combination of deep exfoliation and hydration infusions, with moisture-binding ingredients in high and pure concentrations. These treatments often involve no downtime and leave the skin with an immediate, fresh glow! The first step towards achieving your best skin through in-spa treatments is knowing the basic science behind your skin's current conditions and how the procedure works. Applying your skincare knowledge will help your make the right treatment selections and can make all the difference between no results and "Starlight Skin".

AGING SKIN: LET'S GET FIRM

Skin that's aging has begun to lose collagen and elastin proteins due to decreased fibroblast activity in the dermis. Fibroblasts are the cells responsible for creating collagen and elastin proteins, which give our skin structure and stretch. Beginning in our early twenties, up to 1% of collagen is lost each year if no action is taken. Skin lacking collagen and elastin becomes thin and shows signs of drooping and wrinkling. The body's natural process of skin renewal also slows as the hands of time move on, resulting in a lacklustre complexion. Additionally, aging skin may involve hyper or hypo pigmentation due to accumulative UV exposure, hormonal changes, and overworked melanocytes. Broken or dilated blood vessels causing permanent redness may also be present.

The Main Factors of Aging Skin

1. **Decreased fibroblast activity**, causing collagen and elastin proteins to diminish.

Starlight tips:

Continual stimulation of fibroblasts in the dermal layer of the skin is the key to a complexion that glows long-term. This can be done with regular red-light therapy (20 minutes a day, 5 times a week is the general recommendation), and through consistent exfoliation and facial massage. Adding a micro-current device to your Starlight Step regimen shocks your fibroblasts into action by sending a gentle pulse of energy into your dermal area and will ensure your skin stays as tight as it possibly can. Fibroblast activity can also be activated by using skincare serums containing peptides. Peptides are short chains of amino acids that direct your skin cells to perform certain functions, such as triggering protein creation, and are scientifically manufactured. To further increase collagen, taking a daily supplement of type 1 or 2, hydrolyzed collagen is suggested.

2. **Accumulative free-radical damage.** Free radicals are unstable molecules, usually oxygen, that attack healthy cells and accelerate the aging process.

<u>Starlight tips</u>:

Antioxidants are the number one defender against free radicals, and can be found in nutritious foods and beverages, and in great skincare products. The most common antioxidants in skincare are vitamin C and E, but there are many more. When relying on antioxidants in products, it is vital that they're present in a stable form to ensure efficacy. Look for scientific studies done by skincare companies to prove the shelf life of their products and the quality of their ingredients. To further ensure you're getting adequate amounts of antioxidants maintain a diet rich in vegetables, fruits, and legumes, and add a daily powder full of superfoods such as spirulina and cocoa into your routine.

Consumption of alcohol and polyunsaturated fats found in certain vegetable oils produce free radicals in the body, and therefore should be limited by those who strive to glow for life. Stick to healthier oils such as coconut oil, avocado oil, and olive oil in your quest for Starlight Skin. Ceasing the use of cigarettes and street drugs is also essential, as both are known to destabilize molecules, turning them into free radicals. These unhealthy habits decrease the overall health of body cells and negatively impact all organs, including the skin.

As always, a mineral-based SPF is recommended daily, as it will protect you from free-radical damage cast off from high intensity, artificial lighting and UV wave penetration. Use at least a SPF of 30, and if the sun's rays are intense reapply your lotion every 2 hours and increase the factor level. Remember to keep your favorite pair of UV protective sunglasses nearby to protect the delicate skin around the eye area from harm. For a bronzed glow, stick to spray tans and self-tanning products, instead of destroying your youthful skin in a UV lamp bed.

3. **Slow cell turnover**: As the years pass the skin's natural renewal process declines and dims a once glowing complexion.

Starlight tips:

Retinol is known as skincare's magic ingredient, as it rapidly increases the turnover rate of skin cells, resulting in a vibrant and smooth complexion. Begin with a low-dose retinol as your night serum a few times per week, before increasing frequency and strength with time. Look for a retinol that's combined with soothing and hydrating ingredients, which can decrease the common symptoms associated with retinol adjustment. These symptoms include flaking and dehydration, breakouts, and sensitivities. Retinol is such a powerful anti-aging ingredient that if you neglect to apply it to your neck and chest there will be a noticeable difference between the texture of these areas and your youthful face. When adjusting to retinol you may have to temporarily reduce your regular exfoliation practices as skin will feel sensitized. Cycle exfoliation back into your regimen when able to continue enjoying its vast benefits. Look for a retinol that displays its strength on the bottle to avoid using a product with only trace amounts of the powerhouse ingredient. Be extremely cautious with UV exposure while using retinols, as they cause your skin to become photosensitive, increasing the risk of skin damage.

Professional Medical Spa Treatments for Youthful Skin

Any skincare treatment that deeply exfoliates, hydrates, and nourishes the skin will provide youth renewing effects, however it's the heavy-hitting treatments that produce collagen and elastin proteins in bulk quantities that create the greatest visible improvement. These ultimate treatments include radiofrequency and microcurrent technology, lasers and intense pulsed light, or techniques of ablation and controlled trauma to the skin, which trigger a natural, reparative bodily response. Stem cells, peptides, and nutrient dense formulas can enhance the effectiveness of these medical spa services. Dermal fillers and injectables can also assist you in presenting a youthful face to the world but maintaining a healthy skin regimen alongside these anti-aging aids is an absolute must. Achieving Starlight Skin throughout a lifetime takes commitment and regular visits with your skin professional. Best results are always seen after multiple treatments and with time.

CHAPTER 4

SKINCARE FOR YOUR BODY

Starlight Skin isn't just for your face. The skin on your body deserves to radiate health and vitality as well! Body skin is thicker than facial skin, has more hair follicles with denser hair, has larger volumes of fat cells beneath it that grow and shrink, and normally secretes sebum only in the chest and back areas. Because of these differences specific Starlight processes are recommended to meet the unique conditions your body may face.

Body Acne: Body acne exists in places where natural sebum is excreted from the follicles, which typically include the chest and back. These follicles become blocked the same ways as the pores on the face (from excess oil, an obstructed follicle, and from the existence of p. acne bacteria). Body follicles can also become clogged from rich products designed to treat dry body skin, with ingredients registering on the comedogenic scale.

<u>Starlight tips:</u>

Refer to all applicable advice in the acne section of Starlight Skin and treat your body acne with the same methods. In addition to this, wash your face and acne-prone areas last in the shower to ensure that when you do your following Starlight

Steps there is no pore-clogging residue on your hands from shampoos, conditioners, or body washes. Rich body washes containing ingredients rating on the comedogenic scale are safe for the arms, belly, and lower half of your body in many cases so be sure to wash acne prone areas with a separate product that promotes clear skin. Stubborn body acne requires daily and nightly Starlight Steps, so showering twice a day is often necessary.

Does Sweat Cause Body Acne?

Sweat doesn't directly clog pores, however, it can create a bacteria friendly environment. If a shower and Starlight Steps after your workout isn't possible, refresh acne prone areas with an anti-bacterial toner and a clear skin spot treatment or serum.

Keratosis Pilaris: keratosis pilaris is the cluster of tiny, red, or white bumps that can appear on the back of the limbs and butt area. It's caused by excess keratin, a protein found in the epidermal layers of the skin, creating a plug that sits over the follicle. This condition is hereditary but can be improved.

Starlight tips:

Exfoliate with body washes and lotions containing salicylic acid and alpha hydroxy acids to break down the keratin plugs. Treat this skin as a sensitive area by avoiding all products with added fragrances and dyes as well as harsh mechanical exfoliators. Keeping skin affected by keratosis pilaris hydrated softens the plugs, so moisturizing these areas up to 4 times a day is recommended. This commitment will be rewarded with silky, smooth skin.

Hyperpigmentation: Hyperpigmentation on the body is caused by the same factors that create these unwanted markings on the face. Follow the Starlight advice in "Let's Get Even" to create a uniform complexion head to toe.

Starlight tips:

Always carry sun protection in your bag to reapply to your hands after washing them. Keep sun protection in your car as well to protect you from the UV A rays that come right through car windows. This diligence will prevent sunspots from appearing later in life, and although this may seem like an issue you can deal with in the future, prevention is always better than fixing! Light and breezy fabrics and soft coloured clothing work best in high UV index climates. With these items and accessories, it's possible to create a stylish, sun-safe image without baring your skin to the sun, its number one age accelerator!

Aging Body Skin: Youthful skin is bright, even, firm, hydrated, and soft. If you can work to achieve these traits your skin will never show its true age. To do this collagen and elastin production must be stimulated, cell-turnover sped up, skin must be fed with nutrients and antioxidants, and high-water content must be maintained in the epidermal layers. Therefore, the same Starlight Tips from "Let's Get Firm" are applicable to the skin on the body as well as the face.

Starlight tips:

If you love the experience of relaxing in a tanning bed, make the switch to a red-light LED therapy booth and help your skin instead of hurting it. These can be found at many medical spas and can be purchased for in-home if you can afford the investment and have the space.

For body exfoliation dry brushing is a great option as the brush is a one-time purchase and you can customize the depth and intensity you exfoliate by adjusting the pressure you apply and the length of time you do it. Only dry brush on areas of the skin that are free of acne, inflamed lesions, or irritations. Use a high quality, natural bristled brush to avoid scratchy, synthetic fibres that could do more harm than good. Customize your exfoliation regimen as needed by using multiple exfoliation mediums at different times. If your skin feels rough exfoliate more often, and if the skin is soft or sensitive exfoliate less.

To keep the skin on your body well moisturized use high quality products with health and youth promoting properties. Reapply often and lock the hydration of your quenching products in with an additional seal rating low on the comedogenic scale. Argan oil and shea butter are great sealing options as always. Applying these products when your skin is still damp from the shower adds an extra boost of H20.

Medical spa treatments for glowing, youthful skin can be customized for the body in many cases, so be sure to learn about your options from your trusted skincare professional.

Stretch Marks: Stretch marks form as skin stretches due to weight gain from puberty, hormonal imbalances, a high caloric diet, or pregnancy. When stretch marks are in their early stage, they contain pigment and once mature the pigment fades to white. Stretch marks appear on the skin as an indented, striped texture.

Starlight tips:

Reduce the pigment of young stretch marks with professional phototherapy treatments. The appearance of matured stretch marks can be improved by stimulating fibroblasts with exfoliation, speeding up cell turnover with retinol products, and professional treatments that induce collagen and elastin, resurface, or use ablation techniques.

Avoid excessive weight gain by gathering knowledge of how to feed your body nutritiously, committing to an exercise program that you love, and by reaching out for professional guidance if support is needed to balance emotional eating. You can help your elastin fibres within the dermal layer to increase in numbers by following the "Let's Get Firm" advice, but these proteins can only stretch so much before the evidence of their hard work leaves visible imprints. If you're pregnant then congratulations! Keep your skin on the belly, thighs, and hips hydrated and nourished and focus on enjoying the beautiful process your body is undergoing. You can use the Starlight tips given to diminish the appearance of any well-earned stretch marks later!

Remember that confidence and self love trumps all skin issues and you're only human so will experience many conditions throughout your lifetime. Starlight Skin isn't about perfection it's about practicing great skincare and reaping the rewards!

Cellulite: Cellulite is the dimpled appearance that can occur on areas of the body that store excess fat and is a common skin related complaint. Remember to focus on the factors you have control over and accept the reality of the minor imperfections any human is bound to have.

Starlight tips:

Decreasing excess body fat with a caloric deficit diet and exercise plan helps cellulite ridden areas smooth out, but there are additional measures you can take for those stubborn fat-storage areas like the thighs and butt. To achieve a firm, cellulite free surface in these areas, dry brushing with deep pressure following the natural flow of the body's circulatory system is recommended on a consistent basis. Professional med spa treatments can also yield impressive results and can involve radio frequency, thermal controlled shrinkage of fat cells, laser therapy, and fat freezing technologies.

Varicose Veins: Varicose veins are bulbous, twisted blood vessels that have swollen due to excess blood pooling from malfunctioning valves. They are most often found on the legs and can be caused by a multitude of factors like obesity, constant standing, a sedentary lifestyle, and hereditary factors. While more superficial and small vascular structures like capillaries can be easily cleared with phototherapy, varicose veins require more specialized treatments.

<u>Starlight tips:</u>

Seek the guidance of your trusted medical practitioner to learn about your available options. Common varicose vein treatments include sclerotherapy, where veins are injected with a medicinal solution causing them to collapse, surgical vein removal, and laser ablation of the vessels. Horse chestnut herbal supplements, elevating feet whenever possible, and compression stockings can prevent existing veins from further swelling, but let's be honest the goal is to get rid of these suckers entirely!

Cracked heels: Dry and cracked heels are an issue for many, but great improvement is possible when you give the area some extra TLC. Glow Getters aim to stay smooth from the feet up!

<u>Starlight tips:</u>

Give your heels special care by committing to a regular foot buffing session before your shower. Don't just leave this step to your pedicurist as this extra maintenance is needed to obtain an always soft heel. Use a finely grained foot paddle, a chemical body exfoliant, or an alternative mechanical method that is gentle enough to not cause injury to the skin. Moisturize the area often and as needed apply a rich cream or balm intended for the foot area. Seal this balm in with a comfy pair of socks for additional heel hydration.

Dermal Scarring: If a past injury has left you with scarring don't let it get you down. There are multiple ways to improve the appearance of deep dermal scarring.

Starlight tips:

Resurfacing the skin through exfoliation and boosting cell turnover rates with retinols can be done at home to help this condition, however medical spa treatments will provide more dramatic and quick results. Treatments involving ablation and controlled trauma of the skin that create a natural, reparative response from your body can be highly effective for deep scars. Dermal fillers can also help to fill out permanent skin indentations. Inquire about your available options with your go-to skincare professional.

If a scar is new be sure to feed the tissues with nutritious ingredients and antioxidants, keep the skin hydrated, and once the initial wound recovers boost rejuvenation with red light therapy.

Dermatitis: Dermatitis is an umbrella term to describe skin inflammations which can include hives, psoriasis, eczema, and rashes. Many forms of dermatitis are hereditary but there are extra measures you can take to keep these conditions in check.

Starlight tips:

Keeping skin irritations at bay begins with establishing a strong lipid barrier on the skin's epidermal layer. To do this avoid harsh soaps and astringents, provide your skin with nutrients and moisture, and supplement your body with essential fatty acids. Decreasing your exposure to irritants by using body products and clothing detergents free of fragrances and dyes will also help skin stay calm.

Pay close attention to your skin's response after ingesting certain foods and undergo an allergy test to help you recognize which substances to stay clear of. With autoimmune conditions like psoriasis and eczema flare ups can be caused by psychological stress and the humidity levels of your environment. Remember to think calm and positive thoughts as much as possible and add humidifiers in your home during cold seasons.

Professionals specializing in natural medicine may be able to customize a solution to ease your dermatitis through herbal supplementation or nutritional planning. Be open to educating yourself on all healthy methods of putting your best skin forward.

Unwanted Body Hair & Ingrown hairs: The fight against unwanted body hair brings forth many issues like stubble, ingrown hairs, and follicular edema, a condition where the hair follicle swells and becomes red and irritated. Thank the beauty Gods for laser hair removal! You're lucky to live during a time when safe and effective laser hair removal is available for all skin tones and hair densities with the exception of white, unpigmented hair. Because laser permanently reduces hair growth your skin will be soft and free of the above conditions once you've carried out your sessions.

Starlight tips:

Find a laser clinic with high quality machinery and licenced staff members to carry out your laser hair removal sessions. Your laser technician will schedule your appointments based on the active cycles of your hair growth and will educate you on the proper before and after requirements to ensure optimal results.

To maintain smooth skin between laser sessions or when shaving, waxing, or using other hair removal methods exfoliate often to keep keratin plugs, dead skin cells, and other debris from blocking the pore. Moisturizing the skin on a consistent basis will also improve any skin conditions that coincide with hair removal.

Skin tags and moles: Skin tags and new moles can pop up as you age due to many factors including hormonal changes, friction on the skin, and UV exposure. If a skin tag or mole is cramping your Starlight Skin style apply the advice below!

<u>Starlight tips:</u>

Basic skin tags can be taken care of with over the counter drugstore solutions, but if you're prone to hyper or hypo pigmentation it may be best to seek the advice of your skincare professional. Medical skincare treatments for skintags and moles typically involve cauterization, a technique where the unwanted mass is removed through a controlled burn, surgical excision, or shaving of the tag or mole.

Accepting your moles and renaming them as "beauty marks" is a painless and cost-free way to amend the condition! Beauty is defined by the beliefs in your mind, which have been imprinted over your lifetime by those close to you, media and advertisements, and societal statements. You have the ultimate power over your beliefs and can change them with persistent focus to think in a way that better serves you.

Accept and Love Your Body Now

The Starlight Skin knowledge required to customize and execute your body's ideal skincare routine will improve your skin's appearance, but without self-love and body acceptance your regimen remains incomplete. The vibrations you radiate when you're happy in the present moment are healing and have the power to provide the spark of magic needed to resolve your body's skincare conditions. Be grateful for the amazing abilities your body has and love it, especially since you're bound to it for life!

CHAPTER 5

GLOWING IS A LIFESTYLE

One of the keys to putting your best face forward is glowing from the inside out. This means bringing all areas of your life into harmony, choosing a positive outlook consistently, and constantly moving toward self-improvement. Nourishing your mind, body, and soul and opening yourself to receive the joy you deserve will give you the extra sparkle in addition to your Starlight Skin. To do this identify some of the obstacles in your life that drag you down and put action towards eliminating them. Some common glow-diminishing obstacles include toxic relationships, judging others, partaking in gossip, regret of the past, fear of the future, and dislike of the self. Equip yourself with the tools your need to adapt a radiant persona like good nutrition and self-care, affirmations, meditation or prayer, gratitude, kindness, and a supporting circle of loving friends and family.

There's a direct connection between your emotions and your skin. Does your face flush when you're embarrassed or angry? Does your complexion dull when you've experienced grief or long periods of sadness? Imagine how radiant your glow will be when you feel wonderful on the inside and when you genuinely smile often!

Join the Glowing Skin Tribe: Take the Starlight Vows

Okay Glow Getters, you're now one step away from becoming an official member of Starlight's Glowing Skin Tribe and have the power to increase your vibrational energy and shine!
Raise your right hand to the stars and affirm out-loud:

I vow to always increase my skincare knowledge,
follow the Starlight Steps, and use quality products
that are right for my skin type and conditions.

I vow to never miss a cleanse and to never leave
the house without SPF during daylight.

I vow to share the Starlight Tips with anyone
in need and spread the gift of glow.

I vow to work toward self-love and self-honour in every way.

With these vows I join the Glowing Skin Tribe
and welcome Starlight Skin into my life!

CONCLUSION

Welcome to the Glowing Skin Tribe! We hope that you've enjoyed our book and have found our advice to be clear and helpful. Now's the time to return to the information you've highlighted and build your customized skin-plan on paper. Post this plan on your bathroom mirror or keep it visible where you can refer to it often. As you become confident in your role as a skin expert feel free to tweak your plan and experiment with different products, techniques, tools, professional treatments, nutrition, and affirmations. Remember that your skin speaks to you and you must respond to its moods and changes with the proper care and actions! Please share this book with those close to you and discover our skin-typing quizzes, case studies, products and more at www.starlightskin.ca.

With love,
Kaye and Jessica, The Starlight Girls!

GLOSSARY

Ablation: the complete removal of targeted skin tissue.

Acne: the inflammation and lesions that occur due to a blocked hair follicle with bacteria growth inside.

Antioxidants: free-radical fighting, health promoting compounds.

Blackhead: an acne congestion containing oxidized pus.

Cellulite: A dimpled appearance in the skin of the body, caused by excess fatty tissues stretching over compromised connective tissue.

Collagen: a dermal protein responsible for giving the skin structure and firmness.

Comedogenic: pore clogging.

Comedogenic Scale: a rating system that determines the likeliness of an ingredient to sit within a pore and clog it.

Dehydration: lacking water content.

Dermatitis: an inflammation of the skin that includes many conditions such as hives, psoriasis, eczema, and general skin rashes.

Dermis: the middle layer of the skin where blood vessels, the base of hair follicles, and fibroblasts are located.

Elastin: a dermal protein responsible for giving the skin youthful elasticity and stretch.

Epidermis: the exterior layer of skin which houses melanocytes and has a superficial layer of dead skin cells.

Fibroblast: a specialized dermal cell responsible for producing collagen and elastin proteins.

Follicular edema: Swelling and redness surrounding a hair follicle usually caused by irritants like waxing and shaving.

Free Radical: an unstable molecule that attacks healthy cells.

Glow Getter: one who is on the quest for Starlight Skin.

High Frequency: an energy current that can kill acne bacteria and cause optimal product penetration.

Hyaluronic Acid: a naturally occurring substance in the body that has humectant properties.

Hydroquinone: a medical-grade skin lightening ingredient.

Hyperpigmentation: a skin condition where excess melanin causes pigment deposits in the epidermis.

Hypopigmentation: a skin condition where pigment is non-existent.

Ingrown hair: a hair that bends within the hair follicle causing irritation and a congested pore.

LED Therapy: light emitting diode phototherapy where different wavelengths of the colour spectrum target different conditions of the skin, creating beneficial outcomes.

Lipid Barrier: a layer of fatty acids on the skin's surface that protects it from external irritants, helps in maintaining skin's ideal pH, and aids in water retention.

Melanin: pigment created by melanocytes in the epidermal layers.

Melanocytes: specialized cells in the epidermis that create melanin.

Microneedling: a medical spa treatment where controlled trauma is induced to the skin, causing a reparative, collagen boosting response from the body.

Papule: an inflamed pimple where no pus is present.

Peptides: short chains of amino acids that give directive instruction to body cells.

pH Scale: a rating system to convey the acidity or alkalinity of a substance, in the case of this book the skin's acid mantle.

Post-inflammatory Hyperpigmentation (PIH): dark marks from pimples or skin traumas.

Product Induced Milia: tiny, hard, whitehead like lesions caused by pore clogging products.

Pustule: an inflamed pimple with pus.

Radiofrequency: an energetic current that effectively stimulates collagen and elastin production through stimulation of the fibroblasts.

Resurfacing: removal of the top epidermal layers while simultaneously speeding up cell turnover rates.

Retinol: a medical skincare ingredient derived from vitamin A that is proven to speed up cell turnover rates, mimicking the abilities of young skin.

Rosacea: a skin condition where blood vessels are superficial and broken, and skin is prone to sensitivities.

Sclerotherapy: the injection of a medicinal solution into a vein to rid of it.

Sebum: a natural oil secreted by the skin's sebaceous glands, located in select hair follicles.

Squalane: a moisture-binding skincare ingredient that increase hydration levels.

Starlight Skin: skin that's healthy, smooth, hydrated, and bright.

The Fitzpatrick Scale: a skin casting system based on an individual's response to UV exposure used to assess risks of injury with professional treatments.

The Glowing Skin Tribe: a select group of individuals that follow the Starlight Steps and have taken the Starlight Vows.

The Retinol Uglies: the period of flaking, sensitivities, and breakouts that can occur when adjusting to a retinol.

Trans-epidermal Water Loss (TEWL): dehydration of the skin by water molecules exiting into the outside environment.

Ultraviolet A Rays: harmful radiation from the sun or artificial lighting that can pass through windows and inflict skin damage as deep as the dermal layer.

Ultraviolet B Rays: harmful radiation from the sun or artificial lighting that causes skin to burn and become damaged in the epidermal layers.

Whitehead: an acne lesion that contains unoxidized pus.